The Ministry of
THE
SHOFAR

by
JIM BARBAROSSA

Step by Step Ministries
215 Sauk Trail
Valparaiso, IN 46385
219-762-7589

ISBN 0-9676380-6-2
©Copyright 2000 Jim Barbarossa

What Are People Saying About The Blowing Of The Shofar?

MARION, OHIO —

For many years, we have had the opportunity to be involved in the ministering arts and the Tabernacle of David style worship, in Asia, Europe, Africa and in the United States.

In this season, as never before, we are seeing the effective use of the Shofar in opening the heavens, in spiritual warfare and calling the people of God together for action. The Shofar, in this manner, is truly a weapon of war!

The anointing of the Shofar in worship also has the ability to lift the worshippers into higher dimensions of the presence of God — it is an instrument of soaring for those who desire to worship in Spirit, as well as, in truth!

PROPHETS JIM & JUDY STEVENS
Christian International Network of Churches Representatives
and staff prophets Marion Christian Center, Marion, Ohio

RIVER OF LIFE MINISTRIES —

When Jim blew the Shofar, the Spirit of God hovered over those meetings and we were so blessed.
PASTORS HAL & PHYLLIS CULBERSON

JUBILEE WORD OF FAITH CHURCH —

When Jim blows the Shofar, the anointing falls. Many have been blessed and healed through the blowing of the Shofar. We had one lady in our congregation who was totally healed of a blood clot in her leg when Jim blew the Shofar.

PASTOR TOMMY GILES

HOLY OF HOLIES MINISTRY —

Dear Jim,

I wanted to take this opportunity to reflect back on our last two Holy of Holies meetings. When you blew the Shofar in the church at Freeport, New York, the atmosphere was changed to Holy Spirit air. The people would not stop shouting for their deliverance. Many were set free that night. The walls of Jericho (Freeport) did come crashing down. Your teaching on the Shofar was excellent. The Word of God came alive for those in the sanctuary. I felt we were transferred to Mt. Zion, and the Word of the Lord came forth through your horn.

The following morning when you ministered to the people at Christian Community Church with the Shofar, I saw the healing power of God flowing through their bodies. Many lives were changed that morning.

During our weekend of ministry in Slidell, Louisiana, the fire of God moved through the sanctuary like a wall of fire, as you blew the Shofar. I was personally touched deeply as you ministered to me at the end of the service. You and your wife Carla are a blessing to the body of Christ and to this Ministry.

Thank you for your faithfulness.

GOD BLESS YOU,
DR. STANLEY J. KMET

SANDY VALLEY COMMUNITY CHURCH —

The blowing of the Shofar changed the atmosphere of the church bringing healing and freedom from fear and pride.

PASTOR JIM GREEN

TRI-STATE RIVER OF LIFE —

The climax of the June 2000 Apostles and Prophets Conference in Versailles, Indiana was when Jim blew the Shofar over Bishop & Mom Hamon. <u>The room was flooded with the awesome presence of the Lord!</u>

PASTOR DAN MOORE

NEW HOPE FELLOWSHIP —

When Jim blew the Shofar, the anointing fell and many people received deliverances immediately!

PASTOR STEVE PERRY

WORSHIP MEETING, JUNE 2000 —

My most startling experience with the Shofar came recently as I approached the altar to receive an impartation for the Gift of Evangelist. As I tarried at the altar, Evangelist Jim Barbarossa lifted up the large Shofar and began to trumpet out short, quick blasts in half second intervals. As each blast rang out, my inner being from around my chest area was being jolted. Something was being ripped a little further out of me with each blast of the Shofar. My personal discernment at that time, and now, is that an evil or evil spirits were being blasted out. Praise the Lord!

GOD BLESS YOU!
BROTHER JIM HAMILTON

A.F.C.M. FAMILY REUNION —

When Jim blew the Shofar, a hush came over the crowd. Then spirits begat spirits. The lifting up of sound and spirit started as a low rumble and ascended until it was a crescendo. People were laughing and crying at the same time. I heard many say "something happened" or "I felt something."

During another meeting when Jim blew the Shofar, the group immediately went into high praise with voices and song. He blew the Shofar again and most of the group were so caught up in the spirit they did not even hear the blowing of the Shofar the second time. I asked several and they said "No, Jim didn't" but a few confirmed he had blown the horn the second time. God used him and the Shofar to lift people up to a higher plain.

GOD BLESS.
JERRY MANNING

CAPE COD CHRISTIAN CENTER —

I have grown to appreciate the special gift and anointing that falls through Jim's blowing of the Shofar. My wife had the nagging pain in her lower back healed at the blowing of the Shofar in one of those meetings. Praise God!

PASTOR TIM WHITEHEAD

PORTAGE, INDIANA —

We have had the privilege of attending several services and meetings where Jim and Carla have ministered with and taught on the Shofar. The teachings were highly informative and quite thorough, leaving no doubt that God has anointed and appointed them in this area for such a time as this. The sound of the Shofar is pure and distinct, blessing all who hear it.

BARRY AND JOY DECKARD

FINAL WORD MINISTRY —

The first time we heard Jim blow the Shofar, we were leaving their home. To us it was as if a battle had been won and the victory was being announced. We were so blessed!

The next time we were privileged to hear the Shofar blown was at an A.F.C.M. family reunion. We had just finished singing and a holy hush had come into the room. Jim in obedience to the Holy Spirit blew the Shofar and praise exploded and the Glory of the Lord was almost tangible. The only word I can use for these experiences is awesome.

DALE & PEARL RAATZ

LAPORTE, INDIANA —

When I hear the sound of the Shofar coming from the breath that God has given you, it is anointed of the Holy Spirit and you can feel it in your spirit, soul, and body.

LOVE IN JESUS,
JAN MURRAY

BOLD LION MINISTRIES —

I first met Jim Barbarossa in June of this year at the Apostles/Prophets 2000 Conference, held at Christian International Family Worship Center in Versailles, Indiana.

During the course of the meetings, he blew the shofar. In my national and international ministry, I have many times heard the shofar blown, but none with the clarity and anointing that this man possesses. The shofar became a musical expression of the anointing of the Lord. The effect was inspirational and carried the kiss of the Spirit of God upon it.

IN HIS SERVICE
GLENN MILLER

The Ministry of
The Shofar

God — Why are people being healed when the Shofar is sounded?

'God, why does the atmosphere, or chemistry of a room change when the Shofar is sounded?' These were my questions.

I purchased a Shofar in Israel in May, 1996. In October of 1996, I felt led of the Lord to take it to Africa with us. Just before leaving for Africa, Carla had a dream. In that dream, she was pregnant. We were in a small car and I was taking her to the hospital. On the way to the hospital, I reached under the seat and pulled out this giant Shofar. I then said to her, *"I will blow the Shofar during the birthing process."* In obedience to God, we took and blew the Shofar. The following is part of a letter received after our trip to Africa:

October 1996, Kenya, Africa

Sister Phanice: *"The blowing of the trumpet (Shofar) you brought here didn't just make a noise. It declared 'Victory!' Demons were cast out! Captives were set free! It revealed that God is reigning in our city in a mighty way. Since you left, we have been having wonderful testimonies about healing, deliverance, and people being set free from evil powers. The Holy Spirit is leading people from one point of glory to another.*

Since then, I have blown the Shofar as the Lord leads and, wow, what God does when the trumpet is sounded!"

February 1997, Cold Water, Michigan
"Woman Set Free." She said, *"I have been bound by fear for over 15 years. When the Shofar was sounded that fear left me. I have been set free. I feel so good, I'm free!"*

May 1998, Cleveland, Ohio
A man healed said: *"I have been in pain for over twenty days. I was hurting so much, that I wasn't going to come to church tonight. I only speak Spanish; and when the man (Jim Barbarossa) was speaking I could not understand him. But God spoke to me and said, 'When he blows that horn, something great is going to happen.' As soon as he blew the horn, the pain left my body. I am healed. You see, I can move my arm and shoulder without any pain. God has healed me!"*

September 1998, F.G.B.M.F.I. Dinner Meeting Holland, Michigan
A man healed said: *"I have been having trouble with my legs. When you blew that horn, God healed me!"*

September 1998, F.G.B.M.F.I. Holland, Michigan
Brother Roy: *"I have had pain in my right shoulder for a long time. I could not lift my arm above my shoulder. When you blew the Shofar, the pain left! I can lift my arm without pain. I am healed."*

October 1998, Woman Healed of Back Problem Tulsa, Oklahoma
She had been in pain for 4 years! When the trumpet was sounded, pain left.

November 1998, Healed! No Surgery Needed

We went to Fountain of Life Church in Michigan City, Indiana just for a visit. At the end of the service, a lady came over to us. She said, "When you were here in October, my husband and I came in late for the service. When we were entering the building, we heard the Shofar being blown." Her husband was having a problem with his shoulder and he was going to have surgery on it. Several times throughout the service Jim blew the Shofar. She said, "Each time the Shofar was blown, he felt something happening in his shoulder." He went back to the doctor. They could not find any more problems with his shoulder and they did not need to operate on it. Thank you Jesus, Praise you Jesus. That is good news, Jesus is our healer.

January 1999, Man Healed

"I have had a problem with my tailbone for a long time. I could never sit through one meeting without being in pain. When you blew that Shofar, the pain left my body and I have sat through 4 meetings without pain."

January 1999, Boy Healed

"I had a lump on my chest and was in pain. When the trumpet was sounded, the pain and the lump left."

February 1999, Pain Left When Shofar Sounded! Hinsdale, Illinois

A man had been in pain for many years. Several times during the meeting, I saw him touch the left side of his face. As I blew the Shofar, I saw him grab his face. He came up at the end of the service. He said, *"I had shingles and was in severe pain but when the Shofar was sounded, the pain left. The pain was gone."* **Thank you Jesus!**

March 1999, St. Louis, Missouri

My back was damaged. I would be in pain a lot of the time. During a revival with Evangelist Barbarossa, at the sounding of the Shofar, Jesus healed my back. I thank God for them and their obedience.   D.C.

March 1999, Alabama

A lady had a blood clot in her leg. After the trumpet was sounded, the blood clot was gone.

June 1999, Springfield, Illinois

A ten-year old girl had a restless and nervous attitude. It left her when the shofar was sounded. She has been easier to relate to since that night.

August 1999, Connecticut

A lady had pain in her knees. When trumpet sounded, the pain left.

September 1999, New York

A man had pain from a pinched sciatic nerve for 2 years. When the trumpet was sounded, the pain left.

September 1999, Pulled Hamstring Healed

A young lady was having pain from a pulled hamstring. When the trumpet sounded, the pain left.

October 1999, Neck and Shoulder Healed

A lady had a pain in the neck and the shoulder. When the trumpet sounded, the pain left.

October 1999, Hebron, Kentucky

A lady had ringing in her ears. She was healed when the trumpet was sounded.

October 1999, Ohio
A young man had severe pain in his knees. When the trumpet was sounded, he jumped up and down without pain.

December 1999, Columbus, Ohio
A man had pain in his hand and arm. When the Shofar was sounding, the man was healed. The pain was gone instantly! The man could lift, carry, and do things that he could not, do just moments before.

March 2000, Versailles, Indiana
A lady with neck problems and pain was instantly healed when trumpet sounded.

June 2000, Detroit, Michigan
A lady with back pain was set free as trumpet was sounded.

June 2000, Portage, Indiana
A man said I can't explain it, but when you blew the Shofar during that one song, something happened in me, something was broke. I can't put it into words, but it was good, and it was God.

Testimonial Letters

GLORY TO GOD

October 8-10, 1998

My husband and I took our family to an AFCM conference in Tulsa, OK. My husband and I attended this conference the year before and were blessed by the testimonies of how God was working all over the world. This year we brought our family, mother-in-law, father-in-law, and also a woman and daughter from the church my husband pastors. Tuesday night the first meeting was a lot of the same introducing everyone and what AFCM is all about.

In the morning meetings they have members get in front of everyone and give testimonies on what God is leading them to do and what he has done in their lives. Jim and Carla Barbarossa were the first couple Jim Kaseman (President of AFCM) happened to call up. This is a couple my husband was in touch with, and they were already planning to minister in our church that following month.

Now I had been suffering with lower back problems since the birth of our third daughter. She was on my sciatic nerve the entire time I was pregnant with her. The pain continued to get worse. I was taking up to five extra strength tylenol a day just to get the day started. And with three children (10, 9, 4) I was always going.

Wednesday morning I woke up in the hotel room and was experiencing a lot of pain. I took my three Tylenol hoping I wouldn't have to take any more. I went to the meeting and sat down with no relief at all from the three Tylenol I had taken. That is when Jim Kaseman introduced Jim and Carla Barbarossa. Jim explained how the power of God moves mighty when the Shofar is blown and I was interested because our daughter has blown the Shofar before at our church. He went on to blow it. By then I was in so much pain and ready to receive my healing that when Jim blew the Shofar I felt the warmth come down from my shoulders to my back and I was set Free! The anointing was so strong. When it was blown God moved. I stood up and had no pain and continue to be pain free. *Glory to God!!!*

HALLELUJAH I'M FREE
ROBIN WHITEHEAD

IT IS FINISHED

The last of September, I had come to a very crucial point in my life. Having dealt with some extremely serious health problems for a very long time, I was in a real situation of life or death. I had gotten several prophesies that the devil was trying very hard to kill me, but that I refused to die. But on this day, I could literally feel life draining from my body. I told God that if He didn't do something, I knew that I couldn't hang on to life much longer.

God had just given me a spiritual dream which gave me wisdom and strategy as to how to destroy this enemy once and for all. After crying out to God, I had a vision.

The basis of the vision was that my enemy had been immobilized by the hands of God. The instructions God had given me involved a process that lasted throughout the day and ended at the home of Jim and Carla Barbarossa, directors of Step by Step Ministries. They had no idea what had occurred during the day. As I and other guests sat at their table to have dinner, Jim made the announcement that the Lord had spoken to him at midnight the night before. He had instructed Jim that when we sat at the table to eat, a certain person was to pray and then he was to blow the Shofar. Now please understand that my experience with people blowing the Shofar has been to hear a sound comparable to that of a dying buffalo. This sound, however, was beautiful and supernatural. It's hard to explain in words what flooded my spirit, but it consisted of great peace and glory — the presence of the Lord was very real to me. As if by supernatural means rather than as the result of a decision to do so, I stood to my feet with my hands and face lifted to God. I worshipped Him from the depths of my heart as the sound from the Shofar seemed to bring His glory all around us. Jim seemed to have a supernatural ability to blow the horn an unusually long amount of time. In addition, the tones and slurrings it made were very uncharacteristic of my experience with Shofars. When he had finished, the silence that followed was interrupted when Jim shared with us what the Lord was instructing him to say. He said that the Lord showed him that though he didn't know what it was, that there had been a long, hard battle, but that IT WAS FINISHED. As he repeated several times that it was finished, I knew that God was speaking specifically to me about the battle I had been fighting all my life. After that, Carla brought out two T-shirts to show us which she had just purchased the day before. On them were pictures of Jesus displaying an expression of "victory" and the words: "It is finished". What a wonderful confirmation. Needless to say, a wonderful time of praise followed.

It is now the last of October, and I have never again experienced the extreme physical attacks of the enemy trying to bring death upon me. He is bound. I am continuing to walk through complete healing, but I have no doubt that the enemy who was trying to bring death upon me has been defeated! Please understand that Jim blowing the Shofar is not a magic potion. Sometimes we as Christians try to put God into formulas. If we hear of someone or a method that God works through, we try to make that thing the means and end of our victory. I know that Jim would not have you follow after that. However, how can we explain how God uses certain things? I believe that God is working miracles across the world not through Jim's horn, <u>but through his OBEDIENCE to use the horn as instructed by God</u>. I thank God for His touch, as well as the obedience of Jim and Carla to be led by the Spirit of God.

PASTOR BARBARA BUNTON

God Help Me To Understand!

At this point, I (Jim) had no biblical understanding of the Shofar or what was happening. All I know is when I saw that Shofar, I had to buy it, and that I needed to be obedient and blow it as God leads me. Since then, I have sought God for answers and searched the Bible, and I will do my best to share these things with you.

A Shofar is a horn from an animal, prepared to be used as a musical instrument. Shofars are usually made from the horn of a ram, wild goat, gazelle, antelope or kudu. The horn of a cow is never used because of the golden calf. *(Exodus, Chapter 32)*

Shofar is mentioned about 70 times in the Bible. You will find it as a trumpet, cornet or Ram's Horn.

There are two types of Shofars:

1. Ram's Horn Shofar

2. Yemenite Shofar
(larger of the two, usually 3' to 4' long.)

The Ram's Horn sounds like an animal crying. It is a repentant-type sound. The Yemenite sounds more like a modern trumpet. It has a jubilee sound, a celebration sound.

Sizes of Yemenite Shofars

Jumbo	40" & 45"
Large	36" & 39"
Medium	32" & 35"
Small	27" to 31"

Sizes of Ram's Horn Shofars

Size AA	21" & 24"
Size A	18" to 20"
Size B	15" to 17"
Size C	12" to 14"
Size D	8" to 11"

My personal Yemenite measures 42" long and produces several notes. Most jumbo Yemenite horns that I have tried give 2 or 3 notes. Every horn has a sound of its own. No two are alike. My Yemenite is fully polished and sounds much like a modern trumpet, with very clear, crisp notes. I have found that the unpolished or natural Yemenites usually produce a deeper or lower pitched sound. If you are looking for a good Yemenite, I would recommend a jumbo, but nothing smaller than a large.

If you find that your lips are too big for the standard mouth piece or hole in most Yemenites, you can modify them, but you must be careful not to damage the horn.

I modified my personal horn by cutting off about 1" of the length on the mouth piece end. I then took a cone shaped grinding disk, attached to a drill and widened the end out like the mouth piece of a trumpet.

My personal ram's horn is a size B. It is half polished and half natural and is about 17" long. I have had people tell me it hits them on the inside when it is sounded. It has driven many to their knees in an attitude of heart felt repentance.

One question that I am asked a lot, is *"What do you do about the smell or odor that comes out of a Shofar?"* After trying many things, I have found the best way to eliminate the odor is to seal it in with a polyurethane. Hold the Shofar by the bell or big end and spray high gloss polyurethane in the bell while continually turning it. Let it run out the small end. Do this several times. Then put several light coats on the outside of the horn for a beautiful shine.

To learn more about Shofars go to the website www.theshofarman.com and click on tips on buying a Shofar or questions often asked about Shofars.

How do I learn to blow a Shofar?

Breathe in and blow from your diaphragm. The deeper the breath, the longer you can hold or continue the note. The tighter your lips, the higher the pitch or tone will be. You can change the sound by the way you vibrate your lips.

How do I know when to blow the Shofar?

Read and study all the scriptures in this book so you will know the times that it was used throughout the Bible. Depend on and trust the Holy Spirit to tell you when to blow it.

How do I know when to blow it loud or soft, long or short?

Again, I leave this completely to the Holy Spirit.

What is the key to blowing the Shofar?

The anointing! Pray for the anointing to know when and how to blow it.

How do I know when to blow the Yemenite or the Ram's Horn?

The Yemenite has a jubilee sound, the rams horn has a repentant sound, but again believe and trust the Holy Spirit.

Where can I blow the Shofar?

Anywhere the Holy Spirit leads you to.

One day when Carla and I were checking into a hotel, God said, *'Take your Shofar and blow it over the water on the beachfront.'* You should have seen it. I was dressed in swimming trunks, t-shirt and sunglasses carrying a 3½ foot Shofar on my shoulder, walking up and down the beach. Every 150 feet or so I would blow the Shofar and somebody would walk up to me and ask what kind of horn it was. I would say this is an instrument for worshipping the Almighty God. I would then tell them about Jesus Christ.

Another time, I was eating lunch across from a bar while on a mission trip to Jamaica. God said, *'When you finish eating, walk in front of the bar and someone is going to ask you to blow the trumpet. When you blow it, somebody on the inside of the bar will ask you to come inside and blow it.'*

I walked in front of the bar as God said, and three men stopped me and asked to hear the sound that the horn would make. As soon as I blew it, the manager came out of the bar and asked me to come in and blow it. As I went in, he told me to go up to the front and tell the sound man I was to blow the horn. So I went to the sound man and told him. He said go ahead and blow it. As I started to blow it, he turned off all the music. All you could hear was a crisp, clear note ringing throughout the bar. Every head turned towards me, and people started to applaud. These people were applauding to the releasing of what is like the voice of God coming from the trumpet.

During that week, we saw healings, deliverances, salvations, and much more. As I walked out of that bar, I felt that God said to me, *'This is the most important thing that you have done on this trip.'* I don't understand it all, but I know when you release the sound from the Shofar, you are releasing what is like the voice of God. You are releasing power into the atmosphere.

Remember this! It is not necessary to understand everything God tells you to do, but it is necessary to be obedient!

Is the anointing to blow the trumpet transferable?

Can it be imparted form one person to another?

During one of our meetings, a man came forward to receive prayer. He felt God was calling him to blow the Shofar. He said, *"I do not own a Shofar and I don't have the money to buy one, but something just exploded in me when you blew the Shofar."* As I laid my hands on him, the anointing shot through my hands and he went down on the floor.

At the end of the service , a person made a commitment to send me the money to pay for a large and small Shofar for this man. *When God calls, He provides!*

The following Sunday, his pastor told those in service to be obedient to the Lord and go to someone and minister to them as the Lord leads. God spoke to him to go to a specific person and blow the Shofar over them. *(He did not know that this person was having back problems.)* As he obeyed the Lord and blew the Shofar, that person was instantly healed. Praise God.

> **Wherefore I put thee in remembrance that thou stir up the gift of God, which is in thee by the putting on of my hands.**
> **2 Timothy 1:6**

The gift was imparted when Paul put his hands on Timothy.

Remember this! It was Timothy's job to keep the gift stirred up, to use the gift. Just like Timothy, it is your job to keep the gifts of God in you stirred up and use them.

Is God calling you to blow the Shofar?

<u>Witnessing Tool</u>

We sometimes carry the Shofar when we go shopping. People always ask what it is. I tell them it is an instrument of worship. Then I will usually ask them if they would like to hear it. Everyone always says yes. After I blow it, the peace of God is often felt and then I will tell them about Jesus. I usually carry a testimony on cassette tape or a tract to give people at that point. The Shofar can be an awesome tool for evangelism. It may seem foolish, but it works!

> **For ye see your calling, brethren, how that not many wise men after the flesh, not many mighty, not many noble, are called: But God hath chosen the foolish things**

of the world to confound the wise; and God hath chosen the weak things of the world to confound the things which are mighty;

1 Corinthians 1:26-27

*Is God calling you to
use the Shofar as a witnessing tool?*

*Is God calling you to declare His Glory by blowing
the Shofar on the streets in your community?*

The Shofar — What A Door Opener

One day we carried the Shofar into a store with us. When we got to the cash register to pay for something, a conversation started because of the Shofar. We ended up praying for the lady to receive a healing in her body.

Stopped By A Police Officer

On another occasion we were walking around a town in Wisconsin. A police officer saw the Shofar. He stopped and said, *"Isn't that a Shofar?"* I said, *"Yes, it is. Have you ever heard one?"* He said, *"No."* I asked him if he would like to. He said, *"Sure."* I blew it and started to tell him about Jesus. He was into several types of religion. So I told him how God healed me of what the doctors called an incurrable blood disease. Then, I said to him, *"There is a difference between my God and all the gods and religions that you have told me about."*

I told him your gods are all dead. My God is alive. My God healed me of a disease that man could do nothing about. My God's name is Jesus, and He's alive.

He looked at me and said, you know you're right about that. He's the only one that's alive. We left him a tract and asked him to consider Jesus.

Shofar Crosses Language Barrier

While taking a walk on the beach, we stopped and blew the Shofar. A Japanese family heard it and stopped. We could not understand Japanese, and they could not understand English very well. They signaled me by hand signs to blow the Shofar again. When the trumpet sounded, a blanket of peace covered us. God's Glory surrounded us. They signaled me to blow it again and they said two words that we could understand. "Peace" and "God."

Blanket of Fire

After one of our meetings in Versailles, Indiana, a man came up to me and said, *"When you softly blew the Shofar and waved it across the room, in the Spirit, I could see waves of fire, one after another. It was like a blanket of fire covering the room. I'm not sure why but I felt God wanted me to tell you this."*

As the man spoke God brought to my remembrance two prophetic words that had been spoken over me a few years before: 1) You are going to be a flame thrower for God; 2) You are going to be one of God's fire babies.

Who blows Shofars?

Angels blow the Shofar

And he shall send his angels with a great sound of a trumpet, and they shall gather together his elect from the four winds, from one end of heaven to the other.
Matthew 24:31

<u>*Jesus blows the Shofar*</u>

For the Lord himself shall descend from heaven with a shout, with the voice of the archangel, and with the trump of God: and the dead in Christ shall rise first:
1 Thessalonians 4:16

<u>*God blows the Shofar*</u>

And it came to pass on the third day in the morning, that there were thunders and lightnings, and a thick cloud upon the mount, and the voice of the trumpet exceeding loud; so that all the people that was in the camp trembled. And Moses brought forth the people out of the camp to meet with God; and they stood at the nether part of the mount. And mount Sinai was altogether on a smoke, because the Lord descended upon it in fire: and the smoke thereof ascended as the smoke of a furnace, and the whole mount quaked greatly. And when the voice of the trumpet sounded long, and waxed louder and louder, Moses spake, and God answered him by a voice.
Exodus 19:16-19

The Priest blows the Shofar.

And the sons of Aaron, the priests, shall blow with the trumpets; and they shall be to you for an ordinance for ever throughout your generations.
Numbers 10:8

Who are the Priests?

But ye are a chosen generation, a royal priesthood, a holy nation, a peculiar people; that ye should shew forth the praises of him who hath called you out of darkness into his marvellous light:

1 Peter 2:9

All Christians are Priests.

A Christian can blow the Shofar.

So, God blows the Shofar. Jesus blows the Shofar. Angels blow the Shofar. Man blows the Shofar. It must drive the devil crazy when he hears the Shofar. He does not know who is blowing it. Is it man? Is it an angel? Is it Jesus? Is it the final great blast? Is Jesus returning? Let's blow the Shofar and drive the enemy crazy!

Why is the sound of the Shofar so special?

I was in the spirit on the Lord's day, and heard behind me a great voice, as of a trumpet,

Revelation 1:10

After this I looked, and, behold, a door was opened in heaven: and the first voice which I heard was as it were of a trumpet talking with me; which said, Come up hither, and I will shew thee things which must be hereafter.

Revelation 4:1

The voice of God is like the sound of a trumpet.

Who does the air belong to?

Wherein in time past ye walked according to the course of this world, according to the prince of the power of the air, the spirit that now worketh in the children of disobedience:

Ephesians 2:2

The devil is the prince and power of the air. OK! Now what happens when you blow a Shofar? You release into the air *(the devil's camp)* the sound of the trumpet, which is like the voice of God. Each time you sound it, you are hammering the enemy's camp with the voice of God. That is why the atmosphere of a room changes when the trumpet is sounded. You are clearing the air between you and heaven. You drive back the enemy with each blast of the trumpet.

In the beginning God created the heaven and the earth. And the earth was without form, and void; and darkness was upon the face of the deep. And the spirit of God moved upon the face of the waters. And God said, Let there be light: and there was light.

Genesis 1:1-3

God said, God spoke, God created with his voice. When you blow a Shofar, you are releasing that which is like the voice of God. You are releasing God's power and anointing into the atmosphere.

Why are people healed when the trumpet is sounded?

And if ye go to war in your land against the enemy that oppresseth you, then ye shall blow an alarm with the trumpets; and ye shall be remembered before the Lord

your God, and ye shall be saved from your enemies.

Numbers 10:9

Sickness is of the enemy that oppresseth you. When we blow the Shofar in obedience to the ordinance, God delivers people from the enemies that oppress them *(pain, sickness)*.

What effect does the blowing of the Shofar have on the enemy?

And they stood every man in his place round about the camp: and all the host ran, and cried, and fled. And the three hundred blew the trumpets, and the Lord set every man's sword against his fellow, even throughout all the host: and the host fled to Beth-shittah in Zererath, and to the border of Abelmeholah, unto Tabbath.

Judges 7:21-22

The enemy's camp went into confusion, and they turned on each other with the sword. Blow the Shofar in your city and send the enemy running.

What brought down the walls of Jericho?

So the people shouted when the priests blew with the trumpets: and it came to pass, when the people heard the sound of the trumpet, and the people shouted with a great shout, that the wall fell down flat, so that the people went up into the city, every man straight before him, and they took the city.

Joshua 6:20

The sound of the trumpet and a mighty shout brought down the walls. OBEDIENCE. Doing exactly what God said to do. At the very time He said to do it.

The Shofar is Sometimes a Call for Repentance

Blow ye the trumpet in Zion, and sound an alarm in my holy mountain: let all the inhabitants of the land tremble: for the day of the Lord cometh, for it is nigh at hand;
Joel 2:1

Therefore also now, saith the Lord, turn ye even to me with all your heart, and with fasting, and with weeping, and with mourning: And rend your heart, and not your garments, and turn unto the Lord your God: for he is gracious and merciful, slow to anger, and of great kindness, and repenteth him of the evil.
Joel 2:12-13

Cry aloud, spare not, lift up thy voice like a trumpet, and shew my people their transgression, and the house of Jacob their sins.
Isaiah 58:1

The Shofar is an Instrument of Worship

With trumpets and sound of cornet make a joyful noise before the Lord, the King.
Psalms 98:6

*Praise him with the sound of the trumpet:
praise him with the psaltery and harp.*

Psalms 150:3

Trumpet of the Jubilee — Proclaiming Liberty

*Then shalt thou cause the trumpet of the
jubilee to sound on the tenth day of the
seventh month, in the day of atonement
shall ye make the trumpet sound throughout all your land. And ye shall hallow the
fiftieth year, and proclaim liberty throughout all the land unto all the inhabitants
thereof: it shall be a jubilee unto you; and
ye shall return every man unto his possession, and ye shall return every man
unto his family.*

Leviticus 25:9-10

Silver Trumpet

*And the Lord spake unto Moses, saying,
Make thee two trumpets of silver; of a
whole piece shalt thou make them: that
thou mayest use them for the calling of
the assembly, and for the journeying of
the camps. And when they shall blow with
them, all the assembly shall assemble
themselves to thee at the door of the tabernacle of the congregation. And if they
blow but with one trumpet, then the
princes, which are heads of the thousands
of Israel, shall gather themselves unto
thee. When ye blow an alarm, then the
camps that lie on the east parts shall go*

forward. When ye blow an alarm the second time, then the camps that lie on the south side shall take their journey: they shall blow an alarm for their journeys. But when the congregation is to be gathered together, ye shall blow, but ye shall not sound an alarm.

Numbers 10:1-7

Silver trumpets were primarily used in the tabernacles and, of course, would have been too expensive for the average person. Today the Yemenite would be used in place of the silver trumpet in local churches.

Blowing of the Trumpets

Speak unto the children of Israel, saying, In the seventh month, in the first day of the month, shall ye have a sabbath, a memorial of blowing of trumpets, an holy convocation.

Leviticus 23:24

And in the seventh month, on the first day of the month, ye shall have an holy convocation; ye shall do no servile work: it is a day of blowing the trumpets unto you.

Numbers 29:1

A Reminder of God's Provision

And Abraham lifted up his eyes, and looked, and behold behind him a ram caught in a thicket by his horns: and

*Abraham went and took the ram, and of-
fered him up for a burnt offering in the
stead of his son.*
Genesis 22:13

Beginning of Festivals

*Also in the day of your gladness, and in
your solemn days, and in the beginnings
of your months, ye shall blow with the
trumpets over your burnt offerings, and
over the sacrifices of your peace offerings; that they may be to you for a memorial before your God: I am the Lord your
God.*
Numbers 10:10

Resurrection

*For the Lord himself shall descend from
heaven with a shout, with the voice of the
archangel, and with the trump of God: and
the dead in Christ shall rise first:*
1 Thessalonians 4:16

Warning of Judgement

*If when he seeth the sword come upon
the land, he blow the trumpet, and warn
the people; Then whosoever heareth the
sound of the trumpet, and taketh not
warning; if the sword come, and take him
away, his blood shall be upon his own
head. He heard the sound of the trumpet,
and took not warning; his blood shall be*

upon him. But he that taketh warning shall deliver his soul.

Ezekial 33:3-6

Anointing of a King

And let Zadok the priest and Nathan the prophet anoint him there king over Israel: and blow ye with the trumpet, and say, God save king Solomon.

1 Kings 1:34

And he brought forth the king's son, and put the crown upon him, and gave him the testimony; and they made him king, and anointed him; and they clapped their hands, and said, God save the king. And when Athaliah heard the noise of the guard and of the people, she came to the people into the temple of the Lord. And when she looked, behold, the king stood by a pillar, as the manner was, and the princes and the trumpeters by the king, and all the people of the land rejoiced, and blew with trumpets: and Athaliah rent her clothes, and cried, Treason, Treason.

2 Kings 11:12-14

Jesus Goes Up!

God is gone up with a shout, the Lord with the sound of a trumpet.

Psalm 47:5

New Moon Celebration

Sing aloud unto God our strength: make a joyful noise unto the God of Jacob. Take a psalm, and bring hither the timbrel, the pleasant harp with the psaltery. Blow up the trumpet in the new moon, in the time appointed, on our solemn feast day.

Psalm 81:1-3

Gathering of the Children of Israel

And it shall come to pass in that day, that the Lord shall beat off from the channel of the river unto the stream of Egypt, and ye shall be gathered one by one, O ye children of Israel. And it shall come to pass in that day, that the great trumpet shall be blown, and they shall come which were ready to perish in the land of Assyria, and the outcasts in the land of Egypt, and shall worship the Lord in the holy mount at Jerusalem.

Isaiah 27:12-13

The Seven Trumpets

And the seven angels which had the seven trumpets prepared themselves to sound. The first angel sounded, and there followed hail and fire mingled with blood, and they were cast upon the earth: and the third part of trees was burnt up, and all green grass was burnt up. And the second angel sounded, and as it were a great mountain burning with fire was cast into the sea: and the third part of the sea became blood; And the third part of the creatures which were in the sea, and had life, died; and the third part of the ships were destroyed. And the third angel sounded, and there fell a great star from heaven, burning as it were a lamp, and it fell upon the third part of the rivers, and upon the fountains of waters; And the name of the star is called Wormwood: and the third part of the waters became worm-wood; and many men died of the waters, because they were made bitter. And the fourth angel sounded, and the third part of the sun was smitten, and the third part of the moon, and the third part of the stars; so as the third part of them was darkened, and the day shone not for a third part of it, and the night likewise.

Revelation 8:6-21

And the fifth angel sounded, and I saw a star fall from heaven unto the earth: and to him was given the key of the bottom-less pit. And he opened the bottomless pit; and there arose a smoke out of the pit, as the smoke of a great furnace; and the sun and the air were darkened by rea-son of the smoke of the pit. And there came out of the smoke locusts upon the earth: and unto them was given power, as the scorpions of the earth have power. And it was commanded them that they should not hurt the grass of the earth, neither any green thing, neither any tree;

but only those men which have not the seal of God in their foreheads. And to them it was given that they should not kill them, but that they should be tormented five months: and their torment was as the torment of a scorpion, when he striketh a man. And in those days shall men seek death, and shall not find it; and shall desire to die, and death shall flee from them. And the shapes of the locusts were like unto horses prepared unto battle; and on their heads were as it were crowns like gold, and their faces were as the faces of men. And they had hair as the hair of women, and their teeth were as the teeth of lions. And they had breastplates, as it were breastplates of iron; and the sound of their wings was as the sound of chariots of many horses running to battle. And they had tails like unto scorpions, and there were stings in their tails: and their power was to hurt men five months. And they had a king over them, which is the angel of the bottomless pit, whose name in the Hebrew tongue is Abaddon, but in the Greek tongue hath his name Apollyon. One woe is past; and, behold, there come two woes more hereafter.

Revelation 9:1-12

And I saw another mighty angel come down from heaven, clothed with a cloud: and a rainbow was upon his head, and his face was as it were the sun, and his feet as pillars of fire: And he had in his hand a little book open: and he set his right foot upon the sea, and his left foot on the earth, And cried with a loud voice, as when a lion roareth: and when he had cried, seven thunders uttered their voices. And when the seven thunders had uttered their voices, I was about to write: and I heard a voice from heaven saying unto me, Seal up those things which the seven thunders uttered, and write them not. And the angel which I saw stand upon the sea and upon the earth lifted up his hand to heaven, And sware by him that liveth for ever and ever, who created heaven, and the things that therein are, and the earth, and the things that therein are, and the sea, and the things which are therein, that there should be time no longer: But in the days of the voice of the seventh angel, when he shall begin to sound, the mystery of God should be finished, as he hath declared to his servants the prophets. And the voice which I heard from heaven spake unto me again, and said, Go and take the little book which is open in the hand of the angel which standeth upon the sea and upon the earth. And I went unto the angel, and said unto him, Give me the little book. And he said unto me, Take it, and eat it up; and it shall make thy belly bitter, but it shall be in thy mouth sweet as honey. And I took the little book out of the angel's hand, and ate it up; and it was in my mouth sweet as honey: and as soon as I had eaten it, my belly was bitter. And he said unto me, Thou must prophesy again before many peoples, and nations, and tongues, and kings.

Revelation 10:1-11

And there was given me a reed like unto a rod: and the angel stood, saying, Rise, and measure the temple of God, and the altar, and them that worship therein. But the court which is without the temple leave out, and measure it not; for it is given unto the Gentiles: and the holy city shall they tread under foot forty and two months. And I will give power unto my two witnesses, and they shall prophesy a thousand two hundred and threescore days, clothed in sackcloth. These are the two olive trees, and the two candlesticks standing before the God of the earth. And if any man will hurt them, fire proceedeth out of their mouth, and devoureth their enemies: and if any man will hurt them, he must in this manner be killed. These have power to shut heaven, that it rain not in the days of their prophecy: and have power over waters to turn them to blood, and to smite the earth with all plagues, as often as they will. And when they shall have finished their testimony, the beast that ascendeth out of the bottomless pit shall make war against them, and shall overcome them, and kill them. And their dead bodies shall lie in the street of the great city, which spiritually is called Sodom and Egypt, where also our Lord was crucified. And they of the people and kindreds and tongues and nations shall see their dead bodies three days and an half, and shall not suffer their dead bodies to be put in graves. And they that dwell upon the earth shall rejoice over them, and make merry, and shall send gifts one to another; because these two prophets tormented them that dwelt on the earth. And after three days and an half the Spirit of life from God entered into them, and they stood upon their feet; and great fear fell upon them which saw them. And they heard a great voice from heaven saying unto them, Come up hither. And they ascended up to heaven in a cloud; and their enemies beheld them. And the same hour was there a great earthquake, and the tenth part of the city fell, and in the earthquake were slain of men seven thousand: and the remnant were affrighted, and gave glory to the God of heaven. The second woe is past; and, behold, the third woe cometh quickly. And the seventh angel sounded; and there were great voices in heaven, saying, The kingdoms of this world are become the kingdoms of our Lord, and of his Christ; and he shall reign for ever and ever. And the four and twenty elders, which sat before God on their seats, fell upon their faces, and worshipped God, Saying, We give thee thanks, O Lord God Almighty, which art, and wast, and art to come; because thou hast taken to thee thy great power, and hast reigned. And the nations were angry, and thy wrath is come, and the time of the dead, that they should be judged, and that thou shouldest give reward unto thy servants the prophets, and to the saints, and them that fear thy name, small and great; and shouldest destroy them which destroy the earth. And the temple of God was opened in heaven, and there was seen in his temple the ark of his testament: and there were lightnings, and voices, and thunderings, and an earthquake, and great hail.

Revelation 11:1-19

Calling of the Assembly

Make thee two trumpets of silver; of a whole piece shalt thou make them: that thou mayest use them for the calling of the assembly, and for the journeying of the camps.

Numbers 10:2

Blow the trumpet in Zion, sanctify a fast, call a solemn assembly:

Joel 2:15

Declare ye in Judah, and publish in Jerusalem; and say, Blow ye the trumpet in the land: cry, gather together, and say, Assemble yourselves, and let us go into the defenced cities.

Jeremiah 4:5

Call To Worship

And it came to pass, when he was come, that he blew a trumpet in the mountain of

Ephraim, and the children of Israel went down with him from the mount, and he before them.

Judges 3:27

God's Directive to Gather the People

There shall not an hand touch it, but he shall surely be stoned, or shot through; whether it be beast or man, it shall not live: when the trumpet soundeth long, they shall come up to the mount.

Exodus 19:13

Gathering of God's People

And it came to pass on the third day in the morning, that there were thunders and lightnings, and a thick cloud upon the mount, and the voice of the trumpet exceeding loud; so that all the people that was in the camp trembled. And Moses brought forth the people out of the camp to meet with God; and they stood at the nether part of the mount.

Exodus 19:16-17

Declaration of Victory in War

And Jonathan smote the garrison of the Philistines that was in Geba, and the Philistines heard of it. And Saul blew the trumpet throughout all the land, saying, Let the Hebrews hear.

1 Samuel 13:3

Announcement of God's Presence

So David and all the house of Israel brought up the ark of the Lord with shouting, and with the sound of the trumpet.
2 Samuel 6:15

Giving Thanks

Then I brought up the princes of Judah upon the wall, and appointed two great companies of them that gave thanks, whereof one went on the right hand upon the wall toward the dung gate: And after them went Hoshaiah, and half of the princes of Judah, And Azariah, Ezra, and Meshullam, Judah, and Benjamin, and Shemaiah, and Jeremiah, And certain of the priests' sons with trumpets; namely, Zechariah the son of Jonathan, the son of Shemaiah, the son of Mattaniah, the son of Michaiah, the son of Zaccur, the son of Asaph:
Nehemiah 12:31-35

Stopping A Battle

So Joab blew a trumpet, and all the people stood still, and pursued after Israel no more, neither fought they any more.
2 Samuel 2:28

God's Wrath Scatters the Enemy

But I will send a fire upon Moab, and it shall devour the palaces of Kirioth: and Moab shall die with tumult, with shouting, and with the sound of the trumpet:
Amos 2:2

God Shall Fight For Us

In what place therefore ye hear the sound of the trumpet, resort ye thither unto us: our God shall fight for us.
Nehemiah 4:20

Lord God Blows the Trumpet

And the Lord shall be seen over them, and his arrow shall go forth as the lightning: and the Lord God shall blow the trumpet, and shall go with whirlwinds of the south. The Lord of hosts shall defend them; and they shall devour, and subdue with sling stones; and they shall drink, and make a noise as through wine; and they shall be filled like bowls, and as the corners of the altar. And the Lord their God shall save them in that day as the flock of his people: for they shall be as the stones of a crown, lifted up as an ensign upon his land.
Zechariah 9:14-16

Sending Of Angels

And he shall send his angels with a great sound of a trumpet, and they shall gather together his elect from the four winds, from one end of heaven to the other.

Matthew 24:31

Last Trump

Behold, I shew you a mystery; We shall not all sleep, but we shall all be changed, In a moment, in the twinkling of an eye, at the last trump: for the trumpet shall sound, and the dead shall be raised incorruptible, and we shall be changed.

1 Corinthians 15:51-52

Gathering Of A Clan

But the Spirit of the Lord clothed Gideon with Himself and took possession of him, and he blew a trumpet, and [the clan of] Abiezer was gathered to him.

Judges 6:34 (Amplified)

Deliverance

And it shall come to pass, that when they make a long blast with the ram's horn, and when ye hear the sound of the trumpet, all the people shall shout with a great shout; and the wall of the city shall fall down flat, and the people shall ascend up every man straight before him.

Joshua 6:5

The walls represent bondages. We have seen people delivered from many things when the trumpet blast is accompanied with a great shout.

- Addictions broken *(cigarettes, alcohol, drugs)*
- Healings received
- Pain instantly disappears
- Blood clots dissolved
- Lumps disappear
- Bondage of fear broken
- . . . and much, much more

God is calling SOME to blow the Shofar and He is calling ALL to be human Shofars. To cry aloud, to lift up your voice, to let a dying world know about Jesus.

Cry aloud, spare not, lift up thy voice like a trumpet, and shew my people their transgression, and the house of Jacob their sins.

Isaiah 58:1

Is God calling you to blow the Shofar?

Is God calling you to be a Human Shofar?

What are you going to do about it?

Scriptures about the Shofar

Scriptures containing "TRUMPET"

Exodus 19:13	1 Kings 1:39	Ezekial 33:4
Exodus 19:16	1 Kings 1:41	Ezekial 33:5
Exodus 19:19	Nehemiah 4:18	Ezekial 33:6
Exodus 20:18	Nehemiah 4:20	Hosea 5:8
Leviticus 25:9	Job 39:24	Hosea 8:1
Numbers 10:4	Psalm 47:5	Joel 2:1
Joshua 6:5	Psalm 81:3	Joel 2:15
Joshua 6:20	Psalm 150:3	Amos 2:2
Judges 3:27	Isaiah 18:3	Amos 3:6
Judges 6:34	Isaiah 27:13	Zephaniah 1:16
Judges 7:15	Isaiah 58:1	Zecharia 9:14
Judges 7:18	Jeremiah 4:5	Matthew 6:2
1 Samuel 13:3	Jeremiah 4:19	Matthew 24:31
2 Samuel 2:28	Jeremiah 4:21	1 Corinthians 14:8
2 Samuel 6:15	Jeremiah 6:1	1Corinthians 15:52
2 Samuel 15:10	Jeremiah 6:17	Hebrews 12:19
2 Samuel 18:16	Jeremiah 42:14	Revelation 1:10
2 Samuel 20:1	Jeremiah 51:27	Revelation 45:1
2 Samuel 20:22	Ezekial 7:14	Revelation 8:13
1 Kings 1:34	Ezekial 33:3	Revelation 9:14

Scriptures containing "TRUMPETS"

Leviticus 23:24	Joshua 6:8	Judges 7:22
Numbers 10:2	Joshua 6:9	2 Kings 9:13
Numbers 10:8	Joshua 6:13	2 Kings 11:14
Numbers 10:9	Joshua 6:16	2 Kings 12:13
Numbers 10:10	Joshua 6:20	1 Chronicles 13:8
Numbers 29:1	Judges 7:8	1 Chronicles 15:24
Numbers 31:6	Judges 7:18	1 Chronicles 15:28
Joshua 6:4	Judges 7:19	1 Chronicles 16:6
Joshua 6:6	Judges 7:20	1 Chronicles 16:42

Scriptures containing "TRUMPETS" (cont.)

2 Chronicles 5:12	2 Chronicles 20:28	Nehemiah 12:41
2 Chronicles 5:13	2 Chronicles 23:13	Job 39:25
2 Chronicles 7:6	2 Chronicles 29:26	Psalm 98:6
2 Chronicles 13:12	2 Chronicles 29:27	Revelation 8:2
2 Chronicles 13:14	Ezra 3:10	Revelation 8:6
2 Chronicles 15:14	Nehemiah 12:35	

Scriptures containing "RAM'S HORN"

Joshua 6:4	Joshua 6:6	Joshua 6:13
Joshua 6:5	Joshua 6:8	

Scriptures containing "CORONET or CORONETS"

2 Samuel 6:5	Psalm 98:6	Daniel 3:10
1 Chronicles 15:28	Daniel 3:5	Daniel 3:15
2 Chronicles 15:14	Daniel 3:7	Hosea 5:8

The Shofar Man

In 1996, God called, appointed, and anointed Jim Barbarossa to teach on and blow the Shofar from a Biblical Christian perspective. Since then, Jim has been asked to blow the Shofar to start conferences all over the country. As Jim sounds this ancient Hebrew instrument of repentance, praise, worship, and warfare, the awesome presence of God is experienced and healings, miracles, signs, and wonders follow.

As Carla Barbarossa worships the Lord in dance, the awesome holy presence of God is ushered in, and tears stream down the faces of many.

To schedule The Shofar Man to start your conference or event with the sounding of the Shofar or to teach on the Shofar, call 219-763-2067 or visit our websites at:
www.theshofarman.com
www.step-by-step.org